"Regard man as a mine
rich in gems of inestimable value.
Education can, alone,
cause it to reveal its treasures,
and enable mankind to benefit there from."

Bahá'ú'lláh

Pronunciation Guide©

Persian	English	Pronunciation
اَ	a	ant
آ	á	arm
ب	b	bat
د	d	dog
اِ	e	end
ف	f	fun
گ	g	go
ه	h	hat
ح	h	hat
ی	í	meet
ج	j	jet
ک	k	key
ل	l	love
م	m	me
ن	n	nap
اُ	o	on
پ	p	pat
ق	q/gh*	merci
ر	r	run
س	s	sun
ص	s	sun
ث	s	sun

Persian	English	Pronunciation
ت	t	top
ط	t	top
و	ú	moon
و	v	van
ی	y	yes
ذ	z	zoo
ز	z	zoo
ض	z	zoo
ظ	z	zoo
چ	ch	chair
غ	gh*	merci
خ	kh*	bach
ش	sh	share
ژ	zh	pleasure
ع	'	uh-oh†

*	: guttural sound from back of throat
†	: glottal stop, breathing pause
ّ	: Indicates a double letter
ْ	: Indicates the letter n sound
لا	: Indicates combination of letter l & á (lá)
ای	: Indicates the long í sound (ee in meet)
اِی	: Indicates the long í sound (ee in meet)
(...)	: Indicates colloquial use

Englisi	Farsi		Englisi	Farsi		Englisi	Farsi
A a	اَ ،ؤَ 'alef		M m	م مـمـم mím		Y y	ى يـيـى ye
Á á	آ ا ا 'alef		N n	ن نـنـن nún		Z z	ذ ذـذ zál
B b	ب بـبـب Be		O o	اُ ،ؤُ 		Z z	ز زـز ze
D d	د دـد dál		P p	پ پـپـپ pe		Z z	ض ضـضـض zád
E e	اِ ،ؤِ 		Q q	ق قـقـق qáf		Z z	ظ ظـظـظ zá
F f	ف فـفـف fe		R r	ر رـر re		Ch ch	چ چـچـچ che
G g	گ گـگـگ gáf		S s	س سـسـس sin		Gh gh	غ غـغـغ ghayn
H h	ه هـهـه he		S s	ص صـصـص sád		Kh kh	خ خـخـخ khe
H h	ح حـحـح he		S s	ث ثـثـث se		Sh sh	ش شـشـش shín
Í í	ى يـيـى ye		T t	ت تـتـت te		Zh zh	ژ ژـژ zhe
J j	ج جـجـج jim		T t	ط طـطـط tá		'	ع عـعـع ayn
K k	ک کـکـک káf		Ú ú	و وـو váv			
L l	ل لـلـل lám		V v	و وـو váv			

Letter Guide©

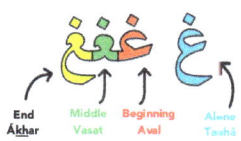

End Ákhar | Middle Vasat | Beginning Aval | Alone Tanhá

The Persian Alphabet

We want to simplify your Persian learning journey as it is such a unique & enigmatic language. There are 32 official Persian letters. The letters change form depending on their position in a word or when they appear separate from other letters. For example, the letter ghayn غ has four ways of being written depending on where it appears in any given word:

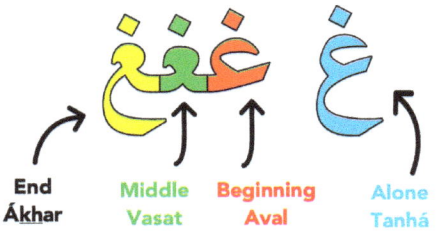

End
Ákhar

Middle
Vasat

Beginning
Aval

Alone
Tanhá

It is important to note that Persian books are read from right to left (←). There are 7 separate or stand-alone letters that do not connect in the same way to adjacent letters (these will not be depicted in red). They are:

Stand alone
Tanhá vámístan

The short vowels a, e & o are usually omitted in literature and are depicted by markings above & below letters (ُ َ). They are not allocated a letter name, unlike their long vowel counterparts á: alef, í: ye & ú: váv (آ ی و).

Caring

Morághebat

مُراقِبَت

á: as (a) in arm

Cleanliness

Nezáfat

á: as (a) in <u>a</u>rm

Compassion

Shafeghat

شَفِقَت

Confidence

Etemád be nafs

اِعتِماد به نَفس

á: as (a) in arm

Consideration

Moláhezeh

á: as (a) in arm

Contentment

Rezáyat

رِضايَت

á: as (a) in arm

Co-operation

Hamkárí

هَمکاری

á: as (a) in <u>a</u>rm
í: as (ee) in m<u>ee</u>t

Courage

Shojáa't

شُجَاعَت

á: as (a) in arm
': glottal stop, breathing pause

Courtesy

Adab
آدَب

Creativity

Kha**lá**gh**í**yyat

خَلاقِیَّت

á: as (a) in <u>a</u>rm
í: as (ee) in m<u>ee</u>t

Determination

Poshte kár

پُشتِ کار

á: as (a) in arm

Detachment

Enghetá'

á: as (a) in arm
': glottal stop, breathing pause

Encouragement

Tashvígh

تَشویق

í: as (ee) in meet

Enthusiasm

E**sh**tí**á**g**h**

اِشتیاق

í: as (ee) in m<u>ee</u>t
á: as (a) in <u>a</u>rm

Excellence

Álí

عالى

á: as (a) in arm
í: as (ee) in meet

Forgiveness

Gozasht
گُذَشت

Friendliness

Dústí

دوستی

ú: as (oo) in m<u>oo</u>n
í: as (ee) in m<u>ee</u>t

Generosity

Bakhshandegí

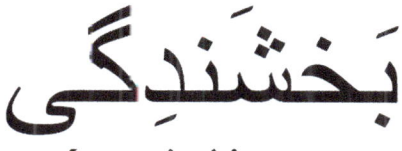

í: as (ee) in m<u>ee</u>t

Gentleness

Moláyemat

مُلایِمَت

á: as (a) in <u>a</u>rm

Honesty

Dorostkárí

دُرُستکاری

á: as (a) in <u>a</u>rm
í: as (oo) in m<u>oo</u>n

Humility

Tavázo'

تَواضُع

á: as (a) in <u>a</u>rm
':   glottal stop, breathing pause

Joyfulness

Shádemání

شادِمانی

(khoshálí)

á: as (a) in arm
í: as (ee) in meet

Justice

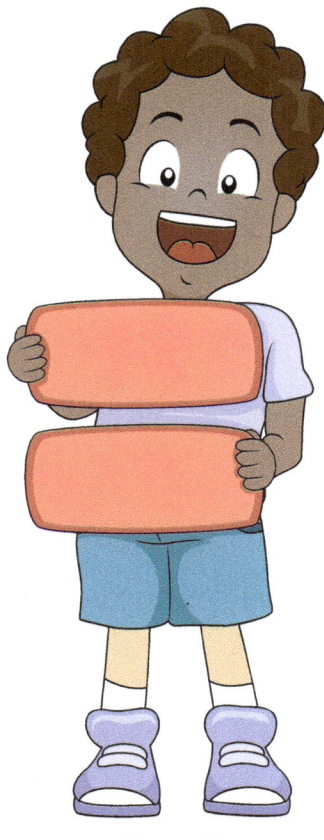

Edálat

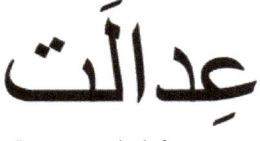

á: as (a) in arm

Kindness

Mehrabání

مِہرَبانی

(Mohabat)

á: as (a) in <u>a</u>rm
í: as (ee) in m<u>ee</u>t

Love

E'shgh

عِشق

Loyalty

Vafádarí

وَفاداری

á: as (a) in arm
í: as (ee) in meet

Modesty

Fúrútaní

ú: as (oo) in m<u>oo</u>n
í: as (ee) in m<u>ee</u>t

Moderation

E'tedál

اِعتِدال

(míyáneh raví)

á: as (a) in arm
í: as (ee) in meet

Obedience

Etáa't

á: as (a) in a̲rm
': glottal stop, breathing pause

Orderliness

Nazm va tartíb

نَظم وَ تَرتیب

í: as (ee) in m<u>ee</u>t

Peacefulness

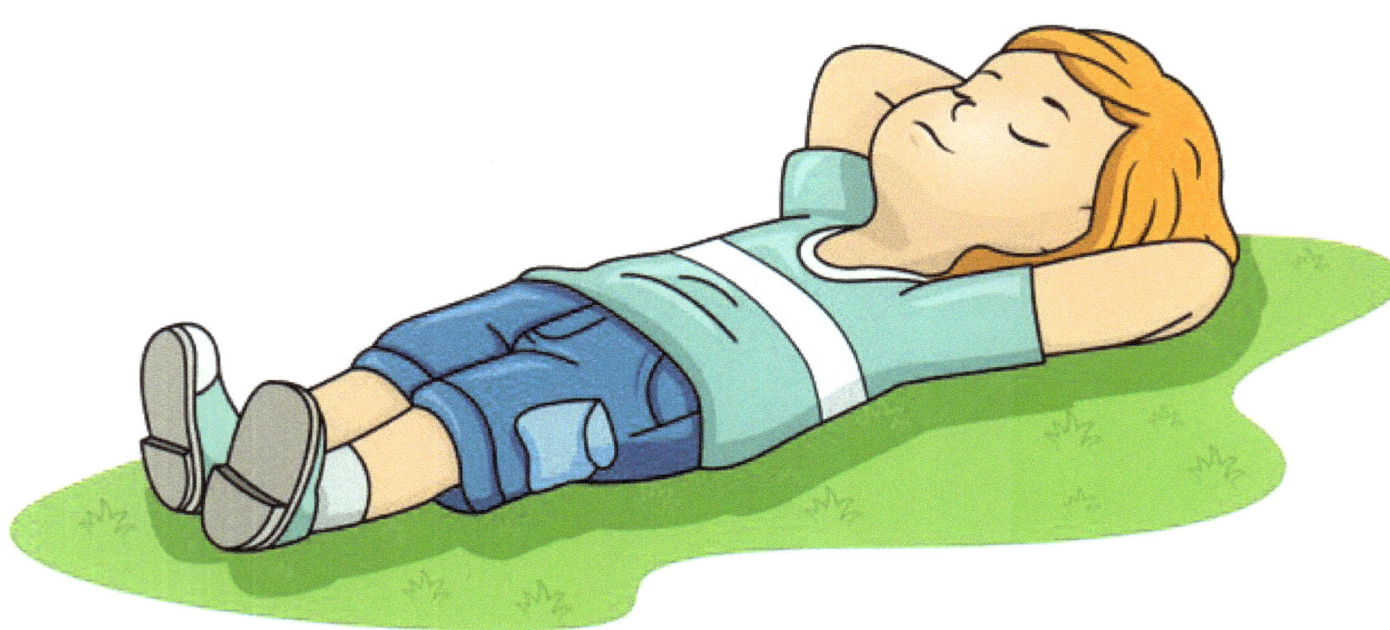

Árámesh

آرامِش

á: as (a) in arm

Respect

Ehterám

a: as (a) in <u>a</u>rm

Responsibility

Masúlíyyat

مَسئولِیَّت

ú: as (oo) in m<u>oo</u>n
í: as (ee) in m<u>ee</u>t

Reverence

Hormat va takrím

حُرمَت وَ تَكريم

í: as (ee) in m<u>ee</u>t

Self Discipline

Khíshtandárí

خویش تَنداری

í: as (ee) in m<u>ee</u>t
á: as (a) in <u>a</u>rm

Helpfulness

Yárí va madad

یاری وَ مَدَد

(Komak kardan)

á: as (a) in arm
í: as (ee) in meet

Thankfulness

Tashakor

تَشَکُر

(Mamnún)

ú: as (oo) in m<u>oo</u>n

Trust

E'temád

á: as (a) in <u>a</u>rm

Truthfulness

Sedághat

صِداقَت

á: as (a) in arm

Unity

Ettehád

اِتّحاد

á: as (a) in <u>a</u>rm

Wisdom

Hekmat
حِكمَت

L

www.ingramcontent.com/pod-product-compliance
Lightning Source LLC
Chambersburg PA
CBHW061750290426
44108CB00028B/2945